STUDENT WORKBOOK

Contemporary Entrepreneurship

Jerry W. Moorman
Professor of Business Administration
Mesa State College
Grand Junction, Colorado

James W. Halloran
Entrepreneur-in-Residence
Business and Accounting Department
Muhlenberg College
Allentown, Pennsylvania

SOUTH-WESTERN EDUCATIONAL PUBLISHING

Cover design by Cindy Beckmeyer, Bruce Design
Cover Illustration by David Tillinghast

Copyright © 1996
by South-Western Educational Publishing
Cincinnati, Ohio

All Rights Reserved

The text of this publication, or any part thereof, may not be reproduced or transmitted in any form or by any means, electronic or mechanical, including photocopying, recording, storage in an information retrieval system, or otherwise, without the prior written permission of the publisher.

ISBN: 0-538-71262-7

1 2 3 4 5 6 7 8 9 EB 99 98 97 96 95

Printed in the United States of America

I(T)P
International Thomson Publishing

South-Western Educational Publishing is a division of International Thomson Publishing Inc. The ITP trademark is used under license.

CONTENTS

INTRODUCTION v

UNIT 1 ENTREPRENEURSHIP AND YOU

Chapter 1	You as an Entrepreneur	1
Chapter 2	Planning the Small Business	5
Chapter 3	Purchasing an Existing Business	9
Chapter 4	Purchasing a Franchise	13

UNIT 2 MARKETING THE SMALL BUSINESS

Chapter 5	Getting to Know Your Customers	17
Chapter 6	Getting to Know Your Competition	21
Chapter 7	Deciding on a Location and Facilities	25
Chapter 8	Developing the Marketing Plan	29
Chapter 9	Pricing and Sales Planning	33
Chapter 10	Promotional Strategies	37

UNIT 3 FINANCING THE SMALL BUSINESS

Chapter 11	Personal Finances	41
Chapter 12	Analysis of Financial Sources	45
Chapter 13	Initial Capitalization and Financial Planning	49

UNIT 4 MANAGING THE SMALL BUSINESS

Chapter 14	Forms of Ownership	53
Chapter 15	Human Resources Management	57
Chapter 16	Management Control Tools	61
Chapter 17	Computer Applications	65
Chapter 18	Small Business Assistance	69

UNIT 5 LEGAL AND ETHICAL CONSIDERATIONS

Chapter 19	Special Regulations	73
Chapter 20	Contracts and Agreements	77
Chapter 21	Buying and Selling	81
Chapter 22	Real Property and Insurance	85
Chapter 23	Ethics and Social Responsibility in Entrepreneurship	89

UNIT 6 CAREERS IN ENTREPRENEURSHIP

| Chapter 24 | International Entrepreneurship | 93 |
| Chapter 25 | Environmental Entrepreneurship | 97 |

Introduction

Just as your student textbook was designed and written with entrepreneurs in mind, so is this *Student Workbook*. It will help your pursuit of entrepreneurship be a rewarding one. This *Student Workbook* is designed to assist you as you master the concepts contained in *Contemporary Entrepreneurship*.

For each chapter, this *Student Workbook* includes clear, straightforward questions to aid you in evaluating your understanding of the concepts in the textbook. The authors have varied the formats of the questions to best approach the subject matter of each chapter.

Following the comprehension questions for each chapter are several activities that your instructor may assign for you to do alone, with a partner, in a small group, or as a class. These activities will challenge you to apply what you already know as you expand your knowledge even further. You may be asked to make use of resources outside of the classroom, such as local newspapers, reference materials, or even local entrepreneurs. Whatever the nature of the activity, each one is designed to further your understanding of issues that may arise when you become an entrepreneur and are running your own business.

Name _____

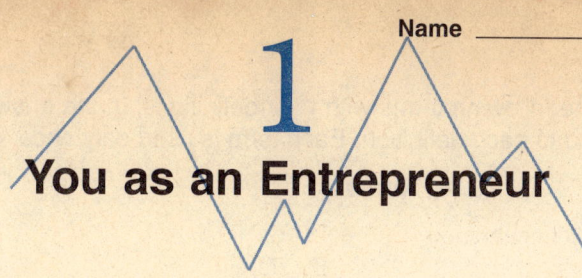

1
You as an Entrepreneur

Study Guide

Part A—*Directions:* In the answers column, write *T* if the statement is true or *F* if the statement is false.

                                                                                                   Answers **For Scoring**

1. All entrepreneurs are small business owners .... _____ _____
2. The right to control one's destiny is the prime motivator for owning a small business .... _____ _____
3. A business plan can be bought at a bookstore .... _____ _____
4. The Small Business Administration is a federal agency in charge of collecting small business taxes .... _____ _____
5. The majority of small businesses fail or close down within five years after opening .... _____ _____
6. A career anchor analysis tells individuals what they are good at doing .... _____ _____
7. Someone with a creative anchor enjoys doing clerical work .... _____ _____
8. People with security anchors do well working in large organizations .... _____ _____
9. An inventor might have an autonomy anchor .... _____ _____
10. VANE is an acronym that stands for variety, action, needs, and excitement .... _____ _____
11. It is a good idea to start a business on a part-time basis before quitting one's job to pursue full-time self-employment .... _____ _____
12. Self-esteem goals refer to the amount of profit a business owner wishes to earn .... _____ _____
13. The phrase *return on investment* refers to how much money a business owner must raise to get a business started .... _____ _____
14. Having a lot of money to invest is the most important determinant in the success of a new business .... _____ _____
15. It is safe for entrepreneurs to assume that the marketplace will be ready for any product or service they wish to offer .... _____ _____

Part B—*Directions:* In the answers column, write the letter of the answer that best completes each statement.

                                                                                  Answers **For Scoring**

1. A person with a managerial anchor would be happy (a)designing a computer program (b)writing a book (c)selling encyclopedias door to door (d)leading a fund-raising campaign for a large nonprofit organization .... _____ _____
2. The acronym VANE stands for (a)value, action, new, energy (b)verify, answer, needs, execution (c)values, attitudes, needs, expectations (d)valuable, activate, noteworthy, exception. _____ _____
3. By recognizing the importance of setting a status goal, aspiring entrepreneurs make certain that (a)their income needs will be achieved (b)they will feel proud of the business endeavor around friends and colleagues (c)the business environment will be one in which they enjoy working (d)travel requirements will be minimal .... _____ _____
4. In deciding how much money it is appropriate to invest in a business, entrepreneurs should (a)calculate how much money they have available by selling all personal assets (b)calculate the money that is available by liquidating assets not needed for personal necessities and supporting their family (c)divide the money they have by two (d)only invest money that banks are willing to lend .... _____ _____
5. The chances of success for a new small business will largely depend on (a)how much money is invested (b)the uniqueness of the idea (c)how much advertising is used (d)the combination of a good business plan and possessing the necessary personal characteristics for success. _____ _____

1

Chapter 1

Part C—*Directions:* Match the following terms with their definitions. In the answers column, write the correct letter on the line next to each definition. Each term is used only once.

Terms

A. Small Business Administration
B. security anchor
C. managerial anchor
D. VANE
E. status

Definitions

	Answers	For Scoring

1. Acronym standing for values, attitudes, needs, expectations .... _____ _____

2. The respect a business owner receives based on how others feel about his or her business. _____ _____

3. A federal agency created to assist the development of the country's small business sector. _____ _____

4. Career anchor characterized by enjoying contact with people and assuming many duties and responsibilities .... _____ _____

5. Career anchor characterized by being happy working in a large organization and needing the assurance of long-term employment .... _____ _____

Activities

1-A. Visit with an established small business owner and discuss how and why he or she decided to open a business. See if you can determine why he or she is successful.
   1. What do you think this person's career anchor is?

   _____

   _____

   _____

   2. Does this person have a business plan?

   _____

   _____

   _____

   3. Does the business meet the values, attitudes, needs, and expectations of this person?

   _____

   _____

   _____

1-B. Visit with your local chamber of commerce to discover the following:
   1. How many new businesses opened in your community during the past year?

   _____

   _____

Chapter 1   Name _____

    2. How does the chamber of commerce assist new businesses?

    3. What future developments are planned for your community?

    4. What other functions does the chamber of commerce perform?

1-C. Obtain recent editions of *Entrepreneur* and *Inc.* magazines. After familiarizing yourself with these publications, summarize how you believe they can be helpful to entrepreneurs.

1-D. Form an entrepreneur's club with at least four fellow students to discuss and investigate types of businesses that would be fun to start. Arrange for weekly meetings to discuss plans on how to start these businesses. At your first meeting, make a list of the businesses you intend to investigate.

Chapter 1

1-E. Form a group with two or three other students. The list on the left names twelve businesses that are relatively easy to start. See how many more you can add. Next, add activities to the second column, listing all the things you like to do. To personalize the list, cross out any items that you do *not* like to do. With the other students, discuss which activities from the list of things you like to do to match the needs of the types of businesses listed.

Types of Businesses	Things You Like to Do
Pet-sitting service	1. Work outdoors
Delivery service	2. Work with my hands
Garage cleaning	3. Computer work
Bicycle repair	4. Talk with people
Party videotaping	5. Entertain others
Computer teacher	6. Be with children
Clown service	7. Use special skills
Typing service	8. Help others
Painting houses/fences	9. _____
Pool service	10. _____
House-sitting service	11. _____
Musician/entertainer	12. _____
_____	13. _____
_____	14. _____
_____	15. _____
_____	16. _____

2 Planning the Small Business

Study Guide

Part A—*Directions:* In the answers column, write *T* if the statement is true or *F* if the statement is false.

		Answers	For Scoring
1.	A business plan is a written outline that guides the entrepreneur to business success	____	____
2.	When purchasing a franchise, a business plan is not necessary	____	____
3.	The business plan is useful only during the design and start-up phases of the business	____	____
4.	The business plan should be consulted regularly	____	____
5.	Starting and maintaining a very small business does not require a business plan	____	____
6.	It is not necessary to develop the business plan until after the entrepreneur has visited the bank	____	____
7.	If a component of the business plan is not applicable to the specific business under consideration, it may be omitted	____	____
8.	A written description of the product or service is not important to a bank	____	____
9.	When goals and objectives are carefully considered, they become the benchmarks along the entrepreneur's path to success	____	____
10.	If goals and objectives are not being met, the entrepreneur should change them to match the business's actual performance	____	____

Part B—*Directions:* In the answers column next to each numbered item, write the letter of the business plan component under which that specific item of information would be included.

- A. concept history and background
- B. goals and objectives
- C. marketing plan
- D. legal requirements
- E. form of ownership
- F. financial plan
- G. organization, management, and staffing plan
- H. special considerations

		Answers	For Scoring
1.	Organizational chart	____	____
2.	Geographic market	____	____
3.	Pricing policy	____	____
4.	Employee requirements	____	____
5.	Personal financial statement	____	____
6.	Consumer profile	____	____
7.	Research and development	____	____
8.	Initial capitalization plan	____	____
9.	Cash flow projection	____	____
10.	Education and training needs	____	____

Chapter 2

Part C—*Directions:* In the blanks provided, write the word or phrase that best completes each sentence.

For Scoring

1. The _____ defines who will be responsible for tasks such as purchasing, advertising, accounting, and hiring personnel. _____

2. The _____ outlines the borrower's education and work experience. _____

3. The _____ describes the borrower's financial condition. In particular, it shows what assets the borrower could use as collateral—something of value pledged as security—for the loan. _____

4. The last component of the business plan deals with any_____ that apply to the entrepreneur's chosen business. _____

5. Once the business plan is complete, the entrepreneur can make the final decision as to whether or not to go into business. The three most useful pieces of information are the _____ _____, the _____, and the _____. _____

Activities

2-A. In your local newspaper, find an article about a small business in your town. Write a brief description of the product or service offered for sale.

_____
_____
_____
_____
_____

What special considerations might this small business owner have had as he or she planned for ownership?

_____
_____
_____
_____
_____
_____
_____

Chapter 2 Name _____

2-B. Choose a small business in your community that you frequent regularly, such as a video rental store or bicycle shop. Use the Yellow Pages of the telephone book to identify other businesses that compete for the same customers. Also, list businesses such as department stores or supermarkets that may be competitors.

_____
_____
_____
_____
_____
_____
_____
_____
_____
_____
_____
_____

2-C. Based on your knowledge of the area in which you live, choose the type of new business that you think has the best chance of being successful. Is it a fast-food franchise, a flower shop, or something completely different? Explain why.

_____
_____
_____
_____
_____
_____
_____
_____
_____
_____
_____
_____
_____

Chapter 2

2-D. Read the newspaper and talk to friends to identify and make a list of businesses in your area that have gone out of business during the last year. Pick one and explain why you think it was not successful.

_____

Imagine that you are going to interview the owner of one of these failed businesses. What questions would you like to ask him or her about the risks of entrepreneurship?

_____

Name _____

3
Purchasing an Existing Business

Study Guide

Part A—*Directions:* In the answers column, write *T* if the statement is true or *F* if the statement is false.

	Answers	For Scoring
1. Business for sale opportunities can be found in classified advertisements in the newspaper.	_____	_____
2. Business sellers often assist buyers in operating a business during the initial stages	_____	_____
3. Sellers sometimes assist in financing the sale of their business	_____	_____
4. The reason a business is for sale is NOT an important consideration to the potential buyer.	_____	_____
5. It is illegal for a business owner to show the business lease to a potential buyer	_____	_____
6. An attorney should draw up a sales contract	_____	_____
7. The goodwill value of a business can be calculated by adding all asset values	_____	_____
8. The earnings approach involves calculating the market value of all assets	_____	_____
9. Liquidation value is a good indication of the return on investment	_____	_____
10. Buyers should NOT expect an immediate change in sales or profits due to new ownership.	_____	_____

Part B—*Directions:* In the answers column, write the letter of the answer that best completes each statement.

	Answers	For Scoring
1. Business brokers are paid a (a)salary (b)specific percentage of the business's selling price (c)sum specified by the seller (d)sum set by the buyer	_____	_____
2. Businesses are frequently sold because of (a)insufficient profits (b)partner or stockholder disputes (c)forced liquidation (d)fear of new competition (e)all of the above	_____	_____
3. Financial records of a business for sale should be analyzed from the past (a)six months (b)year (c)two years (d)three years	_____	_____
4. Bad business opportunities are usually characterized by (a)poor recordkeeping (b)an offer to help train new owner (c)current inventory (d)seller financing	_____	_____
5. When buying a business, buyers should not (a)overestimate the impact a change of ownership will have on the immediate sales and profits of a business (b)use an accountant to verify the financial records (c)negotiate the final price (d)use an attorney to draw up the sales contract	_____	_____

Chapter 3

Part C—*Directions:* Match the following terms with their definitions. In the answers column, write the correct letter on the line next to each definition.

Terms

A. classified advertising
B. earnings approach
C. industry sources
D. market value
E. replacement value
F. seller financing
G. liquidation value
H. negotiation
I. good business opportunity
J. pro forma (projected) income statement

Definitions

1. A business for sale with well-kept records, a profitable history, and, in all probability, a high selling price ....

2. A financial statement that shows the effect of anticipated changes from new management. ....

3. The value of assets if they are sold in an emergency situation or on short notice ....

4. A note paid to the seller of a business as opposed to a conventional lending institution ....

5. Salespeople, suppliers, and members of a trade association ....

6. The cost of buying new assets at current market value ....

7. The final process of determining the price buyers are willing to pay for a business for sale. ....

8. Determining the profits and return on investment of a business for sale opportunity ....

9. Determining the value of a business by researching the value of similar businesses in similar markets ....

10. A place to find business for sale opportunities ....

Activities

3-A. Using personal satisfaction and income objectives as guidelines, review the "Business Opportunities" classified section of a metropolitan newspaper for opportunities that seem to match your objectives. On a separate sheet of paper, write what the advertisements tell you about each opportunity and write any questions you will need to ask the seller. Bring those advertisements, comments, and questions to class. Break into small groups with classmates and present your opportunities.

Chapter 3   Name _____

3-B. Visit a business broker to inquire about opportunities. Ask for a description of how his or her business operates. Request a list of current business opportunities and bring it to class for discussion.

_____
_____
_____
_____
_____

3-C. A business that is for sale for $75,000 has annual sales of $200,000; $50,000 in profits before the owner's salary; and assets of $50,000. Select a classmate to work with, discuss the following questions and write your answers in the space provided.
  1. How would you use the earnings approach to determine the purchase price?

  _____
  _____
  _____
  _____
  _____

  2. What is the goodwill?

  _____
  _____
  _____
  _____
  _____

  3. How would you determine the market value? Replacement value? Liquidation value?

  _____
  _____
  _____
  _____
  _____
  _____
  _____

Chapter 3

3-D. A gift shop costs $25,000 to start from scratch. Or, you could buy one for $50,000, producing a $15,000 profit after the owner's salary. Which situation appeals to you and why?

_____
_____
_____
_____
_____
_____
_____
_____
_____
_____

4 Purchasing a Franchise

Study Guide

Part A—*Directions:* In the answers column, write *T* if the statement is true or *F* if the statement is false.

		Answers	For Scoring
1.	One way to characterize a franchise is as a licensing relationship	_____	_____
2.	One advantage of a franchise is service costs	_____	_____
3.	Franchisors always expect franchisees to pay a percentage of sales	_____	_____
4.	Franchise agreements always impose product or price restrictions on new businesses	_____	_____
5.	One disadvantage of franchising is restricted freedom	_____	_____
6.	Site selection for a franchise may be controlled by the franchisor	_____	_____
7.	The assignment of the franchise is one part of a typical franchise contract	_____	_____
8.	Some franchisors reserve the right to be given the opportunity to repurchase the franchise if the franchisee decides to sell it	_____	_____
9.	Purchase of a franchise never requires renewal	_____	_____
10.	One classification of franchises is retail	_____	_____
11.	Another classification of franchises is vending	_____	_____
12.	A person who has a burning desire to become an entrepreneur and own a small business may have no real idea of what particular business to choose or how to run a business	_____	_____
13.	Franchises currently account for over one-half of the U.S. retail economy	_____	_____
14.	Purchasing a franchise is a desirable option for most entrepreneurs	_____	_____
15.	Coca Cola is a franchise business	_____	_____

Part B—*Directions:* Match the following terms with their definitions. In the answers column, write the correct letter on the line next to each definition.

Terms

A. royalty
B. franchisor
C. franchise
D. franchise broker
E. franchisee

Definitions

		Answers	For Scoring
1.	A right or privilege to conduct a particular business using a specified trade name	_____	_____
2.	A person who buys a franchise from a franchisor	_____	_____
3.	A person or company that offers a franchise to others	_____	_____
4.	An ongoing fee that is paid to the franchisor at specific intervals—usually a percent of gross revenue or net sales	_____	_____
5.	A person who obtains the right from a franchisor to sell franchises within a certain territory	_____	_____

Chapter 4

Part C—*Directions:* List five parts of a typical franchise contract.

_____
_____
_____
_____
_____
_____
_____
_____
_____
_____

Activities

4-A. Using the categories of franchises listed in this chapter, make a list of some franchises or businesses that could be franchises in your community.

_____
_____
_____
_____
_____
_____
_____
_____
_____
_____
_____

Chapter 4 Name _____

4-B. Interview the owner of a franchise in your community. Ask for opinions about the advantages and disadvantages of franchising. Would the owner have purchased the franchise if he or she had it to do all over again? What advice would he or she give to an entrepreneur who is considering a franchise purchase? Take notes in the space provided.

Chapter 4

4-C. Interview a local franchisor and obtain as much information as you can about his or her attitude about franchising. Compare this interview with the franchisee interview and determine where there are similarities and differences of opinion. NOTE: To locate a franchisor, use the sources for finding franchise opportunities that are listed in this chapter.

5 Getting to Know Your Customers

Name _____

Study Guide

Part A—*Directions:* In the answers column, write *T* if the statement is true or *F* if the statement is false.

	Answers	For Scoring
1. Needs are things that individuals feel they must have	_____	_____
2. A market is a group of individuals with unsatisfied needs	_____	_____
3. Shelter is a physiological need	_____	_____
4. A fur coat is a safety need because it is clothing	_____	_____
5. Market research is needed to determine whether there is a community need for the entrepreneur's product or service	_____	_____
6. Collecting information is the first step of market research	_____	_____
7. The *Thomas Register* of industry information is an example of a secondary data source	_____	_____
8. Entrepreneurs should study the needs of the market at least twice a year	_____	_____
9. Current events and changes in the marketplace are not necessary for the final step in the market research process	_____	_____
10. Corporate product development managers often work in the same manner as entrepreneurs.	_____	_____

Part B—*Directions:* In the answers column, write the letter of the answer that best completes each statement or question.

	Answers	For Scoring
1. A market is (a)a central location where goods and services can be exchanged (b)any group of potential customers who have an unsatisfied need for a particular product or service (c)a specialized group of customers with the means to purchase (d)any population of more than 100,000 people	_____	_____
2. Which of the following is NOT one of the need levels in Dr. Maslow's Hierarchy of Human Needs? (a)safety (b)love and belonging (c)financial (d)self-actualization	_____	_____
3. Which of the following is NOT a step used in market research? (a)define the question (b)collect data (c)analyze the data (d)implement data (e)test the results	_____	_____
4. To determine if there is a community need for a product or service, the entrepreneur should start with (a)a survey of potential customers (b)an experimental test market (c)a demographic study (d)a written customer profile	_____	_____
5. A complete demographic study includes (a)the number of people in a marketplace (b)per capita income average of the population (c)the education level of the intended market (d)average age (e)all of the above	_____	_____
6. If the demographic statistics are to be of value, entrepreneurs must (a)make a comparative study (b)test the market (c)survey the market (d)discuss the statistics with the bank	_____	_____
7. If doing industry research, entrepreneurs should collect information regarding (a)the size of the market (b)the number of potential customers (c)how much competition there is (d)whether the market is being serviced adequately (e)all of the above	_____	_____
8. Which of the following is an example of primary data? (a)a telephone survey (b)the encyclopedia (c)an almanac (d)the *Thomas Register* of industry information	_____	_____

17

Chapter 5

9. Which of the following is NOT needed to calculate market potential? (a)population (b)average customer age (c)average spent per capita (d)number of stores .... _____ _____
10. Market research is a (a)tool used to help make decisions (b)method of proving the acceptance of a product or service (c)requirement of the Internal Revenue Service (d)device that must used by all new businesses .... _____ _____

Part C—*Directions:* Match the following terms with their definitions. In the answers column, write the correct letter on the line next to each definition. Each term is used only once.

Terms

A. gender ratio
B. safety needs
C. self-esteem needs
D. economic stability
E. market potential

Definitions   Answers   For Scoring

1. Protection needs such as shelter and clothing .... _____ _____
2. The proportion of each gender to the total population .... _____ _____
3. An economy's ability to withstand changes .... _____ _____
4. The total potential sales dollars for a particular market .... _____ _____
5. Individual needs such as status, recognition, and self-respect .... _____ _____

Activities

5-A. Visit a library or your local chamber of commerce and obtain the following information concerning your community. Use the chart below to record your information.
　1. Current population, population of five years ago, and projected population for five years from now. [Calculate the trend of growth in the past five years by subtracting the population figure of five years ago from the current population figure. Then divide that result by the current population figure to get the trend of growth (in percent).]
　2. Average age and education level (number of years of school attended)
　3. Average annual income per person
　4. Race and gender ratio
　5. Unemployment rate

Obtain the same information for a neighboring community and make a table comparing the two markets.

POPULATION	Five Years Ago	Current	In Five Years	% Change	Average Age	Education	Average Income	Gender Ratio	Unemployment Rate
Your Community									
Other Community									

Chapter 5   Name _____

5-B. Obtain a map of your county and pinpoint the location of the two communities you studied in Activity 5-A. Record the number of residents beside each.

_____

_____

5-C. Contact a sales representative for a nationally distributed product or service (or the home office for a franchise) and obtain the following information.
   1. Average number of inhabitants needed in a community to profitably support the product or service.

   _____

   2. Average amount spent per person, per year, in the product or service classification.

   _____

5-D. Use the community statistics researched in Activity 5-A and the business information obtained in Activity 5-C to analyze the potential success of that business in your community.
   1. If the business is not currently in your community, do you feel it would be a successful addition? List the factors that would make it a good risk or a poor risk.

   _____

   _____

   _____

   _____

   _____

   _____

   _____

   _____

   2. What other data is needed to make a more informed prediction?

   _____

   _____

   _____

   _____

   _____

   _____

   _____

Chapter 5

3. If the business is currently in your community, what factors have made it successful?

   _____
   _____
   _____
   _____
   _____
   _____
   _____

6 Getting to Know Your Competition

Study Guide

Part A—*Directions:* In the answers column, write *T* if the statement is true or *F* if the statement is false.

		Answers	For Scoring
1.	Real business success can only come from having many, many customers	____	____
2.	Knowledge of competition is nice to have but not absolutely necessary for success	____	____
3.	The government decides where consumers can spend their money	____	____
4.	Competition is a very necessary part of private enterprise	____	____
5.	In order for there to be competition, there must be many buyers for a few sellers	____	____
6.	The U.S. government helps ensure fairness in competition	____	____
7.	There are three types of competition	____	____
8.	A physical check of the geographic market is necessary to identify competition	____	____
9.	Direct competition is a term used for companies that are close in location to the competitors.	____	____
10.	Competitors that have failed are of no concern to entrepreneurs	____	____
11.	When using the term *price* in competitive analysis, price range is what is meant	____	____
12.	An entrepreneur should concentrate on a new business's strengths, not its weaknesses	____	____
13.	An effective way to learn what the competition is doing is to simply walk through the competitors' stores and browse	____	____
14.	The Robinson-Patman Act prohibits price discrimination	____	____
15.	Good competitive analysis can prevent most surprises from the competition in the future	____	____

Part B—*Directions:* Match the following terms with their definitions. In the answers column, write the correct letter on the line next to each definition. Terms may be used more than once.

Terms

A. a category for analyzing businesses that have failed
B. a category for analyzing competition in general
C. competition
D. monopoly
E. price discrimination
F. competitor
G. tying agreement
H. competitive analysis

Definitions

		Answers	For Scoring
1.	Identifying and examining the characteristics of a competing firm	____	____
2.	Price level	____	____
3.	Under-capitalization	____	____
4.	Lack of knowledge	____	____
5.	Quality of facility	____	____
6.	When a seller forces a buyer to purchase one product in order to receive another needed or desired product	____	____
7.	Charging different prices to different customers for the same goods	____	____
8.	An individual or business that sells the same products or services as another business and appeals to the same general type of customer	____	____
9.	A market situation in which there is one seller that sets prices	____	____
10.	This element exists when a market has many aggressive sellers	____	____

21

Chapter 6

Activities

6-A. Choose a business area that interests you. Now choose at least four stores or firms that compete in this business. Analyze the different names used and decide if a name can offer a competitive advantage. Rank the names from best to worst.

Name	Rank
_____	_____
_____	_____
_____	_____
_____	_____
_____	_____
_____	_____

6-B. Choose two stores in your town that are in the same business. Cite specific examples of how they try to appeal to their common customer base. Examples might include newspaper, radio, or television ads.

_____
_____
_____
_____
_____
_____

6-C. Imagine that you own a business like the one Laura Watson is opening. A major competitor of yours is a large discount merchandiser. Prepare a list of five reasons a customer should shop with you instead of the much larger store even though your prices are a little higher.

_____
_____
_____
_____
_____
_____
_____
_____

Chapter 6　　　　　　　　　　　　　　　Name _____

6-D. Identify three retail businesses in your area that are direct competitors. You may choose office supply stores, hair salons, or gas or service stations. First, compare the prices of five products or services at each business. Then list these prices in a table such as the one shown below. Note which business tends to have the lowest prices, and which one has the highest. Next, think about other competitive factors, such as customer service, location, the use of coupons, and whether or not the products and services appear to meet the needs of the customers. Write about what you discover. Be sure to draw a final conclusion about which business you believe "beats the competition."

	Product 1	Product 2	Product 3	Product 4	Product 5	Other Factors
Store A	_____	_____	_____	_____	_____	_____
Store B	_____	_____	_____	_____	_____	_____
Store C	_____	_____	_____	_____	_____	_____

Conclusions

_____
_____
_____
_____
_____
_____
_____
_____
_____
_____
_____
_____
_____
_____
_____
_____
_____
_____
_____
_____

Chapter 6

6-E. Interview a local small business owner. Ask the entrepreneur several questions about his or her competition. Summarize the answers in the space below. You may want to use some of these questions, or write your own.
1. Which businesses do you consider to be direct competition for your business? Which ones do you consider to be indirect competition?
2. Do you (or does an employee) actively "shop" or browse around competitive businesses to learn more about them? If so, explain. If not, how do you learn about what the competition is doing?
3. If you started your business all over again, what steps would you take to learn about rival firms during your planning phase?

7 Deciding on a Location and Facilities

Name _____

Study Guide

Part A—*Directions:* In the answers column, write *T* if the statement is true or *F* if the statement is false.

                                                                                                                    Answers   For Scoring

1. Convenience goods are hard to find
2. Shopping goods are very hard to find
3. Specialty goods purchases are usually planned
4. Shopping centers have hurt downtown shopping areas
5. Stand-alone stores are dependent on pedestrian traffic
6. Industrial parks are used for professional offices
7. Incubators are used for storage purposes by large businesses
8. Many part-time entrepreneurs start with home-based businesses
9. The surroundings of a business are important to its image
10. Supermarkets are usually better anchor stores than department stores

Part B—*Directions:* In the answers column, write the letter of the answer that best completes each statement.

                                                                                                                    Answers   For Scoring

1. Convenience will encourage a consumer to (a)buy more (b)buy less (c)be more particular (d)shop less often
2. A toothbrush is an example of a (a)shopping good (b)convenience good (c)specialty good (d)technological product
3. Specialty goods are (a)distributed widely (b)purchased by the rich (c)harder to find than shopping goods (d)available only by special order
4. A diamond ring is an example of a (a)convenience good (b)specialty good (c)shopping good (d)none of the above
5. Downtown shopping areas are often deserted due to (a)the Depression (b)World War II (c)people moving to the suburbs (d)lack of public transportation
6. A shopping center that has fewer than 20 stores and no anchor store is a (a)neighborhood shopping center (b)community shopping center (c)regional shopping center (d)super regional shopping center
7. An entrepreneur who sells impulse merchandise and relies on heavy pedestrian traffic might do well in a (a)stand-alone store (b)neighborhood shopping center (c)regional shopping center (d)deserted downtown area
8. Commercial leases are (a)legal contracts (b)promises to pay for use of space (c)agreed-upon stipulations (d)all of the above
9. The best anchors for shopping centers are usually (a)supermarkets (b)department stores (c)movie theaters (d)restaurants
10. The most important consideration for a location is (a)cost (b)image (c)accessibility (d)structural soundness

Chapter 7

Part C—*Directions:* Match the following terms with their definitions. In the answers column, write the correct letter on the line next to each definition. Each term is used only once.

Terms

A. commercial lease
B. markup
C. super regional shopping center
D. stand-alone store
E. home-based business

Definitions

                          Answers **For Scoring**

1. The difference between what the seller and the consumer pay for a product .... _____ _____
2. A colossal shopping mall comprised of many anchor stores and sometimes hundreds of smaller stores .... _____ _____
3. A store that is not located in a shopping area .... _____ _____
4. A business conducted from the owner's residence .... _____ _____
5. A signed legal agreement that specifies the terms for use of business property by someone other than its owner .... _____ _____

Activities

7-A. Make a list of ten purchases you made recently. Classify each item as a convenience good, a shopping good, or a specialty good. Indicate where each item was purchased—in what store and in what type of shopping area.

Purchase   **Classification**

_____   _____
_____   _____
_____   _____
_____   _____
_____   _____
_____   _____
_____   _____
_____   _____
_____   _____
_____   _____

Chapter 7   Name _____

7-B. Visit local shopping centers. Classify each as a neighborhood shopping center, a community shopping center, a regional shopping center, or a super regional shopping center. Which of these centers do you visit most often? Why?

_____
_____
_____
_____
_____
_____
_____
_____

7-C. Visit a nearby industrial park (inquire about locations at the local chamber of commerce or city hall) and list the tenants. Obtain the following information:
1. In what type of business activity is each tenant engaged?

_____
_____
_____
_____

2. How many square feet does each tenant use?

_____
_____
_____

3. Are there any incubators? If so, list them.

_____
_____
_____

4. Where is the nearest transportation facility?

_____

Chapter 7

7-D. Draw a diagram of a community, regional, or super regional shopping center with which you are familiar. On the diagram, indicate the following:
1. What are your observations about the customer traffic flow?

_____
_____
_____
_____
_____
_____

2. Where are the anchor stores?

_____
_____
_____
_____
_____

3. What would be the best location for a small retail or service business? Why?

_____
_____
_____
_____
_____
_____
_____
_____
_____

8
Developing the Marketing Plan

Study Guide

Part A—*Directions:* In the answers column, write *T* if the statement is true or *F* if the statement is false.

	Answers	For Scoring
1. Determining level of income is an appropriate part of target marketing		
2. The ultimate goal in asking questions for target marketing purposes is to create customer profiles		
3. Market segmentation follows target marketing		
4. Target marketing is used only by small businesses		
5. Almost all entrepreneurs must conduct some basic marketing research		
6. The first step in marketing research is to define the question		
7. Marketing research is necessary only after the business is open		
8. Marketing research should be carried out if a business is experiencing unexpectedly low sales		
9. Primary data is obtained by direct collection		
10. The only way an entrepreneur on a small budget can collect primary data is by observing consumers		
11. The marketing mix variables differ slightly from the four *P's* of marketing		
12. The first part of the communication channel is the message vehicle		
13. "Noise" factors are inhibitors to effective communication		
14. The development of a marketing plan usually results in a list of strategies		
15. The marketing concept is the belief that the business owner's wants and needs drive the market		

Part B—*Directions:* In the answers column, write the letter of the answer that best completes each statement or question.

1. To design a marketing plan for the ideal customer, the entrepreneur must target (a)average purchases (b)the market (c)the competition (d)the best location
2. A description of the ideal customer is called (a)a demographic description (b)a customer profile (c)market segmentation (d)market research
3. The marketing mix includes which of the following? (a)price (b)place (c)process (d)a and b (e)a and c
4. Which of the following is a form of promotion? (a)advertising (b)product (c)marketing research (d)customers
5. Which of the following is/are "noise" factors that distort messages? (a)low volume (b)surrounding noise (c)misspelled words (d)all of these

29

Chapter 8

Part C—*Directions:* Match the following terms with their definitions. In the answers column, write the correct letter on the line next to each definition.

Terms

A. secondary data
B. marketing concept
C. personal selling
D. primary data
E. marketing research
F. target marketing
G. customer profile
H. market segmentation

Definitions

1. The belief that consumer wants and needs are the driving force behind any product development or marketing effort ....
2. Process of dividing the market into groups of similar consumers ....
3. Marketing to a selected group of consumers ....
4. A recorded and complete description of the ideal customer for a business ....
5. Published records are an example of what kind of data? ....

Activities

8-A. Identify two stores in your community that you believe apply the marketing concept to their operations, and two that do not. Explain why you put each store into its category.

Chapter 8   Name _____

8-B. Collect newspaper advertisements from a department store, a restaurant, and a movie theater. Describe the target market you believe the advertisements are intended to attract.

Department store _____

_____

_____

_____

Restaurant _____

_____

_____

_____

Movie theater _____

_____

_____

_____

8-C. Write the customer profile of a frequent viewer of music videos.

_____

_____

_____

_____

_____

_____

_____

_____

_____

_____

_____

Chapter 8

8-D. You want to open a retail music store, but you do not know what kind of music will sell. Develop a short questionnaire and survey at least ten friends or classmates. Ask at least three questions on your questionnaire. Record the results of your research below.

_____

_____

_____

_____

_____

_____

8-E. Find an example of specialty advertising. Identify the item and indicate whether or not you think it helps to increase the business's sales.

_____

_____

_____

_____

_____

_____

8-F. Find four coupons that you think would appeal to college students. Explain briefly what you think the appeal of each coupon is.

_____

_____

_____

_____

_____

_____

9
Pricing and Sales Planning

Study Guide

Part A—*Directions:* In the answers column, write *T* if the statement is true or *F* if the statement is false.

	Answers	For Scoring
1. As prices rise, demand falls	_____	_____
2. In the long run, consumers determine prices	_____	_____
3. Price is a customer relations tool	_____	_____
4. Examples of variable costs are rent, utilities, and insurance	_____	_____
5. Loss of part of a merchandise set is a good reason for taking a markdown	_____	_____
6. Setting prices very high is typical of a status quo pricing strategy	_____	_____
7. Using a market penetration strategy is a method of gaining market share	_____	_____
8. The first part of an effective sale is the sales presentation	_____	_____
9. Publicity is paid advertising	_____	_____
10. Promotional events are forms of referral advertising	_____	_____

Part B—*Directions:* In the answers column, write the letter of the answer that best completes each statement.

	Answers	For Scoring
1. The relationship between supply and demand is part of (a)finance (b)economics (c)advertising (d)accounting	_____	_____
2. In making a purchase to fulfill an unsatisfied need, consumers seek (a)the best bargain (b)utility satisfaction (c)economic satisfaction (d)a total pricing concept	_____	_____
3. The break-even point is reached when (a)a profit is achieved (b)all costs are covered (c)a high markup is used (d)a business is one year old	_____	_____
4. If the cost of a product is $100 and the markup is 60 percent, the selling price will be (a)$160 (b)$250 (c)$60 (d)$140	_____	_____
5. If the markup of an item is 50 percent and the selling price is $200, the cost is (a)$10 (b)$100 (c)$150 (d)$50	_____	_____
6. The total pricing concept refers to (a)the markup percentage (b)sound customer relations and profitable pricing (c)satisfying customer needs (d)utility satisfaction	_____	_____
7. If the cost of a product is $50 and the selling price is $75, the markup percentage is (a)25 percent (b)50 percent (c)33⅓ percent (d)125 percent	_____	_____
8. Sellers take markdowns to (a)increase per-item profit (b)please manufacturers (c)get rid of old merchandise (d)receive tax deductions	_____	_____
9. One part of an effective sale is (a)advertising (b)presentation (c)referral advertising (d)publicity	_____	_____
10. Publicity is one of the marketing tools of (a)a pricing strategy (b)the communication channel (c)a sales plan (d)an economic study	_____	_____

Chapter 9

Part C—*Directions:* Match the following terms with their definitions. In the answers column, write the correct letter on the line next to each definition.

Terms

A. market share
B. markdown
C. publicity
D. sales approach
E. fixed cost

Definitions Answers For Scoring

1. A cost that usually does not change with changes in production and/or sales volume .... _____ _____
2. The difference between the original selling price and the price at which an item is actually sold .... _____ _____
3. The portion of a particular market that uses a particular product or service .... _____ _____
4. The part of the selling process intended to attract the potential buyer's attention and stimulate interest .... _____ _____
5. Advertising that does not incur cost to a seller .... _____ _____

Activities

9-A. Visit a large discount store and a department store and compare the following aspects of business operation.

1. Location—Describe the stores and the businesses that surround them.

   Discount store   **Department store**

   _____   _____

   _____   _____

   _____   _____

   _____   _____

2. Prices—Compare similar products and estimate the overall savings to be obtained at the discount store.

   _____

   _____

   _____

   _____

3. Selection—Does the department store carry a more current selection? Does the discount store offer more variety?

   _____

   _____

   _____

   _____

Chapter 9   Name _____

4. Personnel—Which store has more personnel available to assist shoppers?

   _____
   _____
   _____
   _____

5. Services—What services does the department store offer that the discount store does not?

   _____
   _____
   _____
   _____

6. Why is the discount store able to offer lower prices than the department store? Write your conclusions below.

   _____
   _____
   _____
   _____

9-B. As a manufacturer, you incur fixed costs of $2 and variable costs of $2 per unit produced. You have calculated the break-even point to be 100 units. Draw a break-even graph to illustrate your profit potential.

35

Chapter 9

9-C. Complete the following pricing calculations:
1. Determine the selling price for an item with a cost of $100 and a 50 percent markup.

   _____
   _____

2. Determine the cost of an item with a selling price of $200 and a 40 percent markup.

   _____
   _____

3. Determine the markup percent of an item with a selling price of $15 and a cost of $10.

   _____
   _____

4. Determine the markdown price of an item whose original selling price was $50. Take a discount of 20 percent.

   _____
   _____

9-D. Congratulations! Your school won the state football championship. The student body wants a day off to celebrate the event with a parade through town followed by a dance. You have been chosen to present the request to the school administrators. In the space below, describe your presentation to the school administrators in terms of approach, presentation, and close. Identify possible objections and explain how you would handle them.

_____
_____
_____
_____
_____
_____
_____
_____
_____
_____
_____

10 Promotional Strategies

Study Guide

Part A—*Directions:* In the answers column, write *T* if the statement is true or *F* if the statement is false.

	Answers	For Scoring
1. The most effective promotional strategy is to out-think the competition	_____	_____
2. Businesses should advertise only when they have something new to tell their market	_____	_____
3. New businesses should use competitive advertising strategies when first opening	_____	_____
4. Institutional advertising is used to show the benefits of buying from a particular business.	_____	_____
5. A gas station that advertises in a large metropolitan newspaper is most likely overreaching the intended market	_____	_____
6. The size of a newspaper advertisement is not important as long as the ad is creative	_____	_____
7. Cable television stations can be used by small businesses if the market is carefully targeted.	_____	_____
8. Using the acronym KISS as a guideline for creating an advertisement reminds the advertiser that simplicity is very important	_____	_____
9. To be successful, an advertisement must generate profits that are double the cost of the ad.	_____	_____
10. Sales training programs are used strictly to educate sales personnel on effective selling methods	_____	_____

Part B—*Directions:* In the answers column, write the letter of the answer that best completes each statement or question.

	Answers	For Scoring
1. Advertising the benefits of a particular product is (a)retentive advertising (b)pioneering advertising (c)institutional advertising (d)product advertising	_____	_____
2. Effective advertising is (a)simple (b)personalized (c)consistent (d)targeted (e)all of the above	_____	_____
3. What kind of advertising is used to announce a grand opening? (a)pioneering (b)retentive (c)institutional (d)competitive	_____	_____
4. Radio advertisers should select the stations to use by (a)the number of listeners (b)the best rates (c)the type of listeners (d)the broadcasting power of the station	_____	_____
5. Billboard advertising is particularly effective for (a)movie theaters (b)restaurants and motels (c)jewelry stores (d)small manufacturers	_____	_____
6. The acronym AIDA stands for (a)action, interest, desire, attention (b)attention, intrigue, destiny, action (c)attention, interest, desire, action (d)authority, intensity, dominance, attention	_____	_____
7. The cost of a 5 × 5 newspaper ad at $10 per column inch is (a)$250 (b)$50 (c)$25 (d)$555.	_____	_____
8. The easiest form of selling is (a)cold calling (b)telemarketing (c)retailing (d)product demonstrations	_____	_____
9. To be effective, sales training must (a)emphasize the lowest price (b)motivate salespeople (c)be held in a classroom (d)include audio tapes	_____	_____
10. Promotional events are held to (a)generate customer goodwill (b)introduce new products (c)announce sales events (d)sell seasonal products	_____	_____

Chapter 10

Part C—*Directions:* In the examples below match the advertisement with the type of advertisement. In the answers column, write the correct letter or letters on the line next to each advertisement. More than one type might fit an advertisement.

    A. Product advertisement
    B. Institutional advertisement
    C. Pioneering advertisement
    D. Competitive advertisement
    E. Retentive advertisement

                                            Answers   For Scoring

1. "Grand Opening Today – Come see the latest in swimwear fashions at Aqua World" .... _____ _____
2. "First National has been serving the needs of Bakersville since 1905" .... _____ _____
3. "We guarantee the best prices in town" .... _____ _____
4. "TWP Tires have a 50,000 mile warranty" .... _____ _____
5. "Remember, Nathan's is the only place to shop for a complete selection of stereo equipment" _____ _____

Activities

10-A. Using the acronym AIDA, create a newspaper grand opening advertisement for the Fashion Attic in the space below.

Chapter 10   Name _____

10-B. Write a radio advertisement with an opening statement that illustrates:

A pioneering stage advertisement _____
_____
_____
_____
_____
_____
_____

A competitive stage advertisement _____
_____
_____
_____
_____
_____
_____

A retentive stage advertisement _____
_____
_____
_____
_____
_____
_____

10-C. Bring to class an example of an institutional advertisement and an example of a product advertisement from the morning newspaper.

_____
_____
_____
_____

Chapter 10

10-D. List five promotion ideas that you believe would be effective for an ice cream shop.

_____
_____
_____
_____
_____
_____
_____
_____
_____
_____

11 Personal Finances

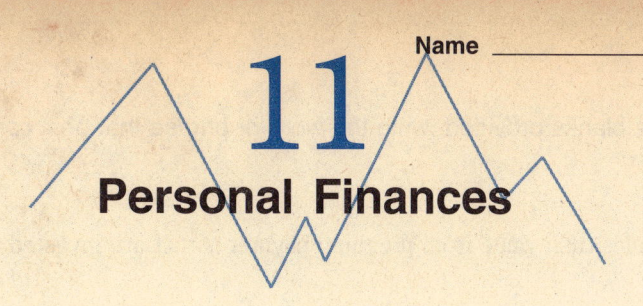

Study Guide

Part A—*Directions:* In the answers column, write *T* if the statement is true or *F* if the statement is false.

1. Good resumés are as many pages long as is necessary to convey all background information.
2. Former supervisors are considered good references
3. All assets owned can be used as collateral
4. A person's net worth is the amount of assets owned
5. Stocks are certificates of partial ownership of companies
6. A bond is a promise to pay a definite amount of money at some future date
7. Public stocks can be converted to cash in a matter of days
8. Home equity is the difference between the appraised value of a house and the amount owed on it
9. The collateral value of stock is greater than its current value
10. Interest or dividends paid on investments that are held as collateral are paid to the lender.
11. Entrepreneurs should expect to be able to obtain all of their capital from a single source

Part B—*Directions:* In the answers column, write the letter of the answer that best completes each statement.

1. A personal resumé is a (a)summary of a person's net worth (b)written description of a person's career accomplishments (c)reference's description (d)document that is included with an individual's tax return
2. A valuable reference is a (a)doctor (b)personal friend (c)former job supervisor (d)relative
3. Resumés should include (a)a photo (b)a summary of educational achievements (c)names of all former supervisors (d)complete descriptions of all positions formerly held
4. A certificate of deposit (a)can be withdrawn without penalty (b)has a lower interest rate than a standard savings account (c)can be used as collateral (d)represents partial ownership in a bank
5. A wise precautionary step for a new business owner is to (a)arrange a regular source of income outside of the business activity (b)invest all available money in the business to show confidence (c)borrow as much money as possible (d)spend all money available to get the business open and presume sales will pay for initial operating expenses
6. Most of the money for a new business comes from (a)bank loans (b)cash on hand (c)investments (d)all of the above

Chapter 11

Part C—*Directions:* In the blanks provided, write the word or phrase that best completes each sentence.

For Scoring

1. An investment that yields cash value from premium payments that are invested is _____ _____. _____

2. Money that an individual owes is _____. _____

3. Assets minus liabilities equals _____. _____

4. A characteristic to avoid when preparing a personal resumé is _____. _____

5. A second characteristic to avoid when preparing a personal resumé is _____. _____

6. A third characteristic to avoid when preparing a personal resumé is _____ _____. _____

7. A fourth characteristic to avoid when preparing a personal resumé is _____, _____, or _____. _____

8. A fifth characteristic to avoid when preparing a personal resumé is _____, _____, or _____. _____

Activities

11-A. Write your own personal resumé on a separate sheet of paper. Highlight school activities and achievements. Also list activities that you pursue outside of school. List all events in chronological order starting with the most recent. At the end of the resumé, list three references who are familiar with your achievements.

11-B. Imagine that you have decided to set up a booth at the next school football game to sell school pennants. The total cost of the materials needed to make the booth and the wholesale cost of 100 pennants is $300. You have $100. How will you come up with the additonal $200?

_____

_____

_____

_____

_____

_____

_____

_____

Chapter 11   Name _____

11-C. The market value of publicly traded stocks is listed in the business section of the newspaper. Look up the following stocks in the listing for the New York Stock Exchange and record yesterday's closing price for each.

American Airlines	_____	General Electric	_____
Eastman Kodak	_____	General Motors	_____
Exxon	_____	IBM	_____
Ford Motors	_____	Walt Disney	_____

11-D. Discuss with a local banker what is considered appropriate collateral for a business loan. What are the main criteria that the bank looks at when considering a small business loan? Summarize what you learn in the space below.

_____
_____
_____
_____
_____
_____
_____
_____
_____
_____
_____
_____
_____
_____
_____
_____
_____
_____

12 Analysis of Financial Sources

Name _____

Study Guide

Part A—*Directions:* In the answers column, write *T* if the statement is true or *F* if the statement is false.

	Answers	For Scoring
1. Banks are the only sources of capital	_____	_____
2. Owner capital and equity capital mean the same thing	_____	_____
3. If an entrepreneur has no personal savings to invest in a business, the dream of the business should be forgotten	_____	_____
4. Venture capitalists specialize in proposals that are not usually acceptable to a bank	_____	_____
5. Venture capitalists should be the first source of funding considered	_____	_____
6. One of the main reasons an entrepreneur would want a partner is for capital purposes	_____	_____
7. Debt capital and creditor capital are the same	_____	_____
8. A local bank qualifies as a private investor	_____	_____
9. Most states have allocated money for new business start-ups	_____	_____
10. The SBA was established in 1953 to aid in the development of small businesses	_____	_____

Part B—*Directions:* In the blanks provided, write the word or phrase that best completes each sentence.

For Scoring

1. Capital borrowed from a lending institution for investment in a new business is called _____. _____

2. Stock or government securities pledged as security for a loan are _____. _____

3. A voluntary association of two or more persons to carry on as co-owners of a business for profit is a _____. _____

4. Capital injected directly into a business from the owner's personal savings is called _____. _____

5. Investors who have excess income available for investment purposes in highly speculative new businesses are called _____. _____

6. A type of financing that allows delayed payment for merchandise is _____. _____

7. Loans made to business owners using real estate property as collateral are called _____. _____

45

Chapter 12

8. A preapproved, prearranged amount of money that a bank will allow a small business owner to borrow is a _____.

9. A loan that requires payments on a regular periodic basis is called an _____ _____.

10. One government source of assistance and financial aid is the _____ _____.

Part C—*Directions:* In the answers column, write the letter of the answer that best completes each statement.

                                                                                      For
                                                                     Answers   **Scoring**

1. Bank loans are a source of (a)equity capital (b)venture capital (c)debt capital (d)private investors .... _____ _____
2. Venture capitalists invest in businesses that (a)are relatively risk free (b) are at least three years old (c)have the potential to produce extraordinary profits (d)have two or more partners. _____ _____
3. A prearranged, preapproved loan that is available to business owners on request is a(n) (a)line of credit (b)installment loan (c)inventory loan (d)collateral loan .... _____ _____
4. The SBA lends money to new business owners through (a)the Internal Revenue Service (b)chambers of commerce (c)banks (d)state and local development offices .... _____ _____
5. A method of raising equity capital is to (a)sell stock (b)take a partner (c)use personal savings (d)all of the above .... _____ _____

Activities

12-A. Determine whether there are any state or local sources of financial assistance for a new small business in your community. List them below.

_____

_____

_____

_____

_____

_____

_____

_____

_____

Chapter 12 Name _____

12-B. Contact the loan department of a local commercial bank and acquire a loan application package. Make some notes below about what the package includes. Are there any questions that you did not expect to see on a loan application? Bring the package to class and discuss the required components.

Chapter 12

12-C. Choose three friends or relatives. Convince each person that you want to start a small business, such as a T-shirt printing business or a concession stand for school sports events. Then ask for a $100 loan to get started. Record their responses and comments below. Bring the results to class for discussion.

13 Initial Capitalization and Financial Planning

Name _____

Study Guide

Part A—*Directions:* In the answers column, write *T* if the statement is true or *F* if the statement is false.

                                                    Answers   **For Scoring**

1. To discover how much money is needed for a business start-up, the starting place is a visit to the bank ....
2. Knowing the inventory turnover rate helps entrepreneurs calculate operating expenses ....
3. New business owners should have three months of operating expense money available before opening ....
4. Pro forma financial statements are necessary only if the entrepreneur plans to borrow money.
5. Cash flow analysis is used to determine net profits ....
6. Current assets are easily converted into cash ....
7. Property is considered a fixed asset ....
8. Sales minus cost of goods minus operating expenses equals net worth ....
9. Accountants are used by entrepreneurs to negotiate contracts ....
10. If business owners hire an accountant, they do not need to maintain their own bookkeeping systems ....

Part B—*Directions:* In the answers column, write the letter of the answer that best completes each statement.

                                                    Answers   **For Scoring**

1. Pro forma financial statements are used to determine (a)the net worth of the business owner (b)the projected financial success or failure of a business enterprise (c)the amount of capital needed to start a business (d)the taxes owed by a business for the past year ....
2. If the inventory turnover of a business is three, the minimum inventory on hand for a business that sells $210,000 per year would be (a)$630,000 (b)$63,000 (c)$70,000 (d)$30,000. ....
3. In addition to capital needed to purchase initial inventory, the owner should have money available for three months of (a)rent (b)salaries (c)utilities (d)supplies (e)all of the above. ....
4. Projected cash flow analyses are used to (a)determine capital needs (b)project a business's financial status (c)indicate how money enters and leaves a business (d)determine advertising needs ....
5. Current assets are (a)easily converted to cash (b)hard to convert to cash (c)short-term liabilities (d)the same as net worth ....
6. Devices that show how much money is required to pay one-time opening costs and to establish an operating reserve are (a)balance sheets (b)capital needs statements (c)pro forma income statements (d)cash flow statements ....
7. Fixtures and equipment of a business are (a)current liabilities (b)current assets (c)long-term liabilities (d)fixed assets ....
8. Accounts receivable are (a)current assets (b)fixed assets (c)long-term liabilities (d)current liabilities ....

Chapter 13

9. The net worth of a business can be calculated as (a)liabilities minus assets (b)assets minus liabilities (c)sales minus costs (d)all of the above .... _____ _____
10. Sales journals are used to record (a)expenses (b)capital purchases (c)receipts (d)accounts payable .... _____ _____

Part C—*Directions:* Match the following terms with their definitions. In the answers column, write the correct letter on the line next to each definition.

Terms

A. undercapitalization
B. current asset
C. leasehold improvements
D. sales journal
E. accountant

	Definitions	Answers	For Scoring

1. The failure of a business to obtain the needed resources to successfully complete its financial objectives .... _____ _____
2. The renovation performed on a store or business to appeal to its customers .... _____ _____
3. Property that is easily converted into cash .... _____ _____
4. An individual trained in the methods and procedures used in assimilating and maintaining financial records .... _____ _____
5. A record of receipts for business activity .... _____ _____

Activities

13-A. Make a personal income statement that shows the money you normally expect to receive each month from your allowance, job, or other sources, and the expenses you normally pay out, such as for lunch, movies, and other purchases. Use the space below.

Income

    Allowance $ _____

    Work $ _____

    Other $ _____

Total income $ _____

Less expenses

    Lunch $ _____

    Entertainment $ _____

    Other $ _____

Total expenses $ _____

Surplus or deficit $ _____

What you have left is the same as a business's profit. It may be used for retained earnings (savings) or for additional purchases.

Chapter 13   Name _____

13-B. Visit an accountant and learn exactly what they do. Would this type of career interest you? Why or why not?

_____
_____
_____
_____
_____
_____
_____
_____
_____
_____
_____
_____

13-C. Visit a stockbroker and request copies of financial statements of large companies that sell stock to the public through the stock market. Compare at least three to determine which one is the most profitable and which one has the greatest net worth. Notice that the statements are in the same format as that of small businesses. What could you, as a small business owner, learn from these statements?

_____
_____
_____
_____
_____
_____
_____
_____
_____
_____
_____
_____

Chapter 13

13-D. Discuss with a local banker what financial information that bank requires before granting a loan to a small business. Make a list here of the requirements and why each item is needed by the bank.

14 Forms of Ownership

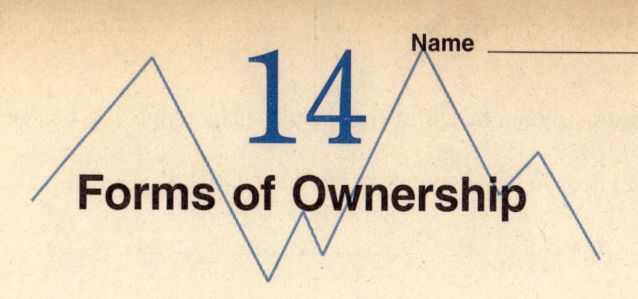

Name _____

Study Guide

Part A—*Directions:* In the answers column, write *T* if the statement is true or *F* if the statement is false.

	Answers	For Scoring
1. A key decision for any entrepreneur is one of ownership	_____	_____
2. If you want to operate a business by yourself, you will be running the business as the sole proprietor	_____	_____
3. A partnership involves three or more people	_____	_____
4. A sole proprietorship may have hundreds of employees	_____	_____
5. The number of employees often determines the type of ownership	_____	_____
6. Partnerships in all states operate under the Uniform Partnership Act	_____	_____
7. One of the first things to do when forming a partnership is to develop a partnership agreement.	_____	_____
8. Partnership agreements are required by law	_____	_____
9. The two major types of partnerships are general and limited	_____	_____
10. A corporation is considered foreign only if it operates outside of the United States	_____	_____
11. The people who start a corporation are called promoters	_____	_____
12. If a store has a name like "Dana Simpson's Video to Go," the name usually must be registered.	_____	_____

Part B—*Directions:* In the blanks provided, write the word or phrase that best completes each sentence.

For Scoring

1. A business established, owned, and controlled by a single person is a _____. _____

2. According to the Uniform Partnership Act, an association of two or more persons to carry on as co-owners of a business for profit is a _____. _____

3. Individuals who voluntarily agree to conduct a partnership are _____. _____

4. An official document stating the contract between partners is a _____. _____

5. A partner who actively engages in the daily management of the business and is fully liable for any actions for, by, and against a business is a _____. _____

53

Chapter 14

6. A partner who does not actively engage in the daily management of a business and has liability limited to the extent of his or her investment in the business is a _____. _____

7. A legal entity created by law is a _____. _____

8. The persons who start the process to create a corporation are _____. _____

9. An application asking the state for permission to form a corporation is called the _____. _____

10. A document that allows a new corporation to do business in a designated state is a _____. _____

11. A share of ownership in a corporation is acquired by purchasing _____. _____

12. The amount of ownership held in a corporation is determined by the number of _____ of stock available. _____

13. People who own stock in a company are called _____. _____

Activities

14-A. Determine what the requirements are for starting a sole proprietorship in your community. Take notes on your findings in the space below. Discuss the requirements in class and determine whether you think they are simple or complex.

_____

_____

_____

_____

_____

_____

_____

_____

_____

_____

_____

_____

_____

Chapter 14   Name _____

14-B. Choose a small business in your community with which you are familiar. Set a time to visit with the owner or owners for an informal interview. Use the questions below as guidelines for your interview. You may wish to take notes on a separate piece of paper. Then write your answers in the space below after the interview.
1. What form of ownership is used?

_____

_____

_____

2. Why did the business owner choose that form of ownership?

_____

_____

_____

_____

_____

_____

_____

3. Would he or she choose the same form if starting over again? Why or why not? Be prepared to discuss your findings in class.

_____

_____

_____

_____

_____

_____

_____

_____

_____

_____

14-C. Contact the official in your state who is responsible for issuing charters to new corporations. Request a copy of the requirements for forming a corporation in your state. Review the information you receive. Bring the requirements to class for discussion.

Chapter 14

14-D. Contact the official or government agency in your state or county that is responsible for registering business names. Request a copy of registration procedures. In the space below, summarize or briefly explain the process involved in business name registration.

_____
_____
_____
_____
_____
_____
_____
_____
_____
_____

15 Human Resources Management

Study Guide

Part A—*Directions:* In the answers column, write *T* if the statement is true or *F* if the statement is false.

		Answers	For Scoring
1.	Only large businesses need organization charts		
2.	A bookkeeper is an example of a staff position		
3.	Many people are more interested in job content than in pay		
4.	Small business owners should be more concerned with employee skills than with their personal characteristics		
5.	Theory X managers often presume that workers dislike their work		
6.	Douglas MacGregor ranked job satisfaction factors in order of importance		
7.	Hygiene factors motivate employees to greater performance		
8.	Rigid personnel rules are essential for small businesses		
9.	An employer who uses top-down management often does not listen to employees or customers.		
10.	Minimum wages were established by the Fair Labor Standards Act of 1938		

Part B—*Directions:* In the answers column, write the letter of the answer that best completes each statement.

1. To determine how many employees can be hired, new business owners should (a)divide the number of hours the business is open by 40 (b)multiply the sales projection by the industry payroll percentage standard (c)hire the same number employed by the competition (d)not hire anyone until the business has been open for one month

2. Sales personnel are (a)staff employees (b)auxiliary employees (c)line employees (d)command employees

3. Employment agencies are helpful because they (a)help screen applicants (b)provide free services (c)do all interviewing (d)pay business owners from money received from applicants

4. When managers closely monitor employee progress towards accomplishing goals, they are (a)directing (b)motivating (c)controlling (d)planning

5. Satisfaction with the work itself is considered a (a)hygiene factor (b)Maslow need (c)motivator (d)Theory Y factor

6. Performance evaluations are (a)organization tools (b)staffing tools (c)directing tools (d)control tools

7. The law that prohibits discrimination based on sex, race, color, religion, or national origin is the (a)Fair Labor Act (b)Civil Rights Act (c)Age Discrimination in Employment Act (d)Occupational Safety and Health Act

8. Pay is considered a (a)hygiene factor (b)control tool (c)motivator (d)job dissatisfier

Chapter 15

9. Businesses that set goals through bottom-up management are successful at (a)controlling (b)listening (c)performance evaluations (d)motivating .... _____ _____

10. Frederick Herzberg is well known for his study of (a)job satisfaction factors (b)Theory X versus Theory Y management styles (c)hierarchy of human needs (d)performance evaluation forms .... _____ _____

Part C—*Directions:* Match the following terms with their definitions. In the answers column, write the correct letter on the line next to each definition.

Terms

A. hygiene factors
B. controlling
C. line organization
D. Theory Y manager
E. Civil Rights Act

Definitions
                                  Answers   For Scoring

1. A business in which all employees are directly involved in performing duties related to the stated mission of the organization .... _____ _____
2. A manager whose primary concern is human relations .... _____ _____
3. Work environment considerations that are expected by employees but do not motivate them. _____ _____
4. Periodic review of employee progress in job-related activities .... _____ _____
5. Prohibited discrimination in employment .... _____ _____

Activities

15-A. Review the help wanted advertisements in your local newspaper and list any that interest you. In the space below, explain why a particular job opportunity appeals to you.

_____

_____

_____

_____

_____

15-B. Choose a partner and take turns in the roles of job interviewer and applicant. Imagine that the open position is in retail sales. You and your partner can decide on the specific product or service. List the questions that you as the interviewer would ask of the applicant. What questions would you as an applicant ask of a potential employer?

Interviewer's questions _____

_____

_____

_____

_____

Chapter 15   Name _____

Applicant's questions _____
_____
_____
_____
_____
_____

Once your lists of questions are complete, conduct your interviews. Do you think that you gathered enough information? How do you think you might improve your next interview?

_____
_____
_____
_____
_____

15-C. Choose a partner and take turns in the roles of the employee being evaluated and the evaluator. Create a hypothetical situation that requires the evaluator to point out some areas in which objectives are not being met. Make note of the following:

1. Is the approach positive or negative?
   _____

2. How does the employee being evaluated react to criticism?
   _____
   _____
   _____

3. Are objectives discussed and agreed upon?
   _____
   _____
   _____

4. How does the session end?
   _____
   _____
   _____
   _____

Chapter 15

15-D. In the space provided below, draw an organization chart for your school's administration. What are the staff positions and the line positions? Are your professors staff employees or line employees?

16 Management Control Tools

Study Guide

Part A—*Directions:* In the answers column, write *T* if the statement is true or *F* if the statement is false.

	Answers	For Scoring
1. Management by objectives is used in large and small businesses	_____	_____
2. The starting place for making a purchase plan is calculating markdowns	_____	_____
3. Keeping an approximate running count of inventory on hand is a perpetual inventory control	_____	_____
4. Telemarketing is an effective method of making a sales presentation	_____	_____
5. If sales are $5,000 more than planned, inventory will be $5,000 more than planned	_____	_____
6. C.O.D. terms are favorable to a 2/10/n30 term of sale	_____	_____
7. Beginning inventory + purchases + sales − markdowns = ending inventory	_____	_____
8. Small businesses are not able to use a just-in-time inventory control system	_____	_____
9. A small business owner should buy computer hardware first and then shop for software that is compatible	_____	_____
10. Small businesses should be more concerned with preventing theft than catching thieves	_____	_____

Part B—*Directions:* In the answers column, write the letter of the answer that best completes each statement or question.

	Answers	For Scoring
1. Business owners should monitor sales results (a)daily (b)annually (c)semi-annually (d)when convenient	_____	_____
2. Counting available inventory by hand is called a (a)perpetual inventory (b)just-in-time system (c)physical inventory (d)hand inventory	_____	_____
3. If a business owner is paying for inventory at the time it is received, he or she is paying (a)2/10/n30 (b)R.O.G. (c)E.O.M. (d)C.O.D.	_____	_____
4. When actual sales differ from objectives, this will NOT affect (a)personnel scheduling (b)inventory levels (c)promotional events (d)utility costs	_____	_____
5. Insurance premiums will increase if (a)sales increase (b)personnel increases (c)rent increases (d)inventory increases	_____	_____
6. Just-in-time inventory system means (a)counting inventory on a regular basis (b)receiving inventory as close as possible to the time it is sold (c)seasonal inventory (d)buying inventory with flexible terms of sale	_____	_____
7. Inventory purchases can be made via (a)trade shows (b)the telephone (c)catalog ordering (d)all of the above	_____	_____

Chapter 16

8. If beginning inventory is worth $10,000 and purchases for the period total $8,000, what is the ending inventory if sales are $4,000 and markdowns are $400? (a)$13,600 (b)$22,400 (c)$6,400 (d)$12,400 .... _____ _____

9. Building a loyal team of employees is important to help control (a)inventory levels (b)employee theft (c)advertising expenditures (d)maintenance costs .... _____ _____

10. A purchase plan must (a)remain rigid (b)contain advertising allowances (c)be flexible (d)be included in annual tax reports .... _____ _____

Part C—*Directions:* Match the following terms with their definitions. In the answers column, write the correct letter on the line next to each definition.

Terms

A. E.O.M.
B. networking
C. physical inventory
D. hardware
E. return on investment

Definitions

                                                                                               Answers   For Scoring

1. The percentage of money invested that becomes profit .... _____ _____

2. An actual count of all inventory on hand .... _____ _____

3. Making personal contact with people who can assist in business development .... _____ _____

4. Computer equipment and accessories .... _____ _____

5. Payment due at the end of the month .... _____ _____

Activities

16-A. List your personal objectives for the next week. Write down the day and time by which each should be completed. How will you monitor your progress toward the objectives?

_____

_____

_____

_____

_____

_____

_____

_____

_____

_____

Chapter 16   Name _____

16-B. Design a purchase plan for your next trip to the grocery store. Take an inventory of groceries on hand and determine what items you wish to bring home. List the purchases necessary to achieve the final objective. Keep a list of what is being consumed during the week (seven days) that follows. By doing this, you will be keeping a perpetual inventory. In the space below, explain how this system could help you save money on groceries.

_____

_____

_____

_____

_____

_____

_____

_____

_____

_____

_____

_____

16-C. Talk to a store manager or law enforcement officer. Discuss the best ways to prevent shoplifting. Also, discuss other crime prevention measures to combat counterfeit money, credit card fraud, and other common crimes against businesses. Write your findings in a page-long report.

Name _____

17
Computer Applications

Study Guide

Part A—*Directions:* Match the following terms with their definitions. In the answers column, write the correct letter on the line next to each definition.

Terms

- A. central processing unit (CPU)
- B. hard disks
- C. printer
- D. computer hardware
- E. monitor
- F. spreadsheet
- G. keyboard
- H. telecommunications
- I. disk drive
- J. floppy disks
- K. mouse
- L. computer literacy
- M. word processing
- N. electronic mail
- O. software

Definitions
Answers | For Scoring

1. The possession of basic competence in the use of common software programs and familiarity with the functions of computer hardware components .... _____ _____
2. The computer equipment that you use .... _____ _____
3. A computer program that accomplishes certain applications or functions *or* translates user's commands to the computer hardware .... _____ _____
4. The part of the computer where all activity takes place *or* the main component of a computer hardware system .... _____ _____
5. The communication of information by computer via telephone lines, cables, or satellite ..... _____ _____
6. Round metal plates that are used to store information and are coated with a magnetic surface .... _____ _____
7. Round plastic sheets that are used to store information and are coated with a magnetic surface .... _____ _____
8. The part of computer hardware that provides a video display of data .... _____ _____
9. The piece of hardware that typically uses alphanumeric keys to input data into the computer. _____ _____
10. Controls cursor movement on the screen and has no keys .... _____ _____
11. The device that generates a hard (paper) copy of information stored in the computer .... _____ _____
12. Creating, processing, printing, distributing, and filing documents through the use of technology. _____ _____
13. Device used to store and retrieve data and programs on disks .... _____ _____

Part B—*Directions:* In the blanks provided, write the word or phrase that best completes each sentence.

For Scoring

1. _____ is the computer equipment.   _____

2. Information that is collected forms the _____ .   _____

65

Chapter 17

3. _____ gathers, stores, and retrieves data. _____

4. The designing and production of a newsletter on a personal computer is _____

   _____. _____

5. _____ programs tell the computer what to do. _____

6. _____ stores telephone messages on a computer disk for later

   retrieval. _____

7. Using technology to create, process, print, distribute, and file documents is _____

   _____. _____

8. A _____ translates written material into electronic signals and

   transmits them over a telephone line. _____

9. The _____ is the part of hardware made up of the control unit and the

   arithmetic/logic unit. _____

10. One way of arranging financial data is to create a _____. _____

Activities

17-A. Write a brief report describing how computers are used in the classrooms at your school, a school you are familiar with, or a school you have read about. Computers are also used for administrative functions. Find out how computers are used for grade reporting, attendance, accounting, and inventory control.

_____

_____

_____

_____

_____

_____

_____

_____

_____

_____

Chapter 17   Name _____

17-B. Choose at least three computer retailers in your community and visit their stores. Compare the various prices for the same computer hardware. Also compare follow-up services after the initial purchase. Develop a chart that displays all the data and present it to your class along with a recommendation of the store that you think offers the best deal.

_____
_____
_____
_____
_____
_____
_____
_____
_____
_____

17-C. Each particular program on the market has its own unique combination of features. The purpose of this activity is to make you familiar with desktop publishing software available for your use. Contact a firm in your community that sells desktop publishing software and ask the following questions.
1. What hardware is popular for use with desktop publishing?

_____
_____

2. What pointers should be kept in mind when selecting software and hardware for desktop publishing?

_____
_____
_____
_____

3. Can *Windows*-based computers be used effectively for desktop publishing?

_____
_____
_____
_____

Chapter 17

17-D. Determine at least three business organizations in your community that use voice mail. Call each business and listen to their voice mail systems. Compare the three and report back to your class on the following.
1. Which was the easiest to understand?

2. Which seemed the most user-friendly?

3. Which was the most frustrating to use?

4. What recommendations would you make to each company regarding their voice mail systems?

18 Small Business Assistance

Name _____

Study Guide

Part A—*Directions:* In the answers column, write *T* if the statement is true or *F* if the statement is false.

	Answers	For Scoring
1. There is little support and assistance for small business owners	_____	_____
2. College professors provide SBA counseling services	_____	_____
3. The United States Department of Commerce grants patents, U.S. trademarks, and U.S. service marks	_____	_____
4. Results of Bureau of Economic Analysis studies are published annually	_____	_____
5. Entrepreneurs can contact the Bureau of the Census for information about rules that pertain to business	_____	_____
6. SBDC programs are cooperative ventures between the SBA and state business development departments	_____	_____
7. The State Sales and Use Tax Division issues identification numbers to retail businesses	_____	_____
8. Becoming a member of a chamber of commerce is a good way to make contacts with other business owners	_____	_____
9. SCORE counselors charge a fee for their services	_____	_____
10. Accountants offer assistance in reviewing leases	_____	_____

Part B—*Directions:* In the answers column, write the letter of the answer that best completes each statement.

	Answers	For Scoring
1. The SBA was created to help small businesses with (a)financial needs (b)counseling (c)advocacy (d)all of the above	_____	_____
2. The Bureau of the Census is a (a)state agency (b)community agency (c)federal agency (d)private company	_____	_____
3. The Office of Business Liaison develops and promotes a cooperative working relationship between the U.S. Department of Commerce and the (a)Office of the President (b)leaders of foreign countries (c)business community (d)state and local governments	_____	_____
4. The Economic Development Administration was established to (a)protect existing jobs (b)generate new jobs (c)stimulate commercial and industrial growth (d)all of the above	_____	_____
5. Small Business Development Centers are funded by (a)private corporations (b)local governments (c)federal and state governments (d)colleges and universities	_____	_____
6. The SBDC Connection is (a)an international trade center (b)a central small business library (c)an office for minority small business development (d)a government procurement office	_____	_____
7. If a small business owner has a question regarding workers' compensation, he or she should call the (a)chamber of commerce (b)Federal Trade Commission (c)State Department of Labor (d)Office of the Secretary of State	_____	_____
8. An entrepreneur who is considering starting a new business and wishes to learn about the local market should first visit (a)the chamber of commerce (b)a local accountant (c)city hall (d)an attorney	_____	_____

Chapter 18

9. Small Business Development Centers offer (a)counseling (b)educational seminars (c)loan application assistance (d)all of the above .... _____ _____

10. Incorporation procedures are administered through the (a)SBA (b)Department of Commerce (c)Office of the Secretary of State (d)Federal Trade Commission .... _____ _____

Part C—*Directions:* Match the following terms with their definitions. In the answers column, write the correct letter on the line next to each definition.

Terms

A. accountant
B. attorney
C. chamber of commerce
D. insurance agent
E. Small Business Development Center

Definitions   Answers   For Scoring

1. Federal/state cooperative agency that assists small businesses through counseling and education. _____ _____
2. A person who assists and advises regarding financial matters .... _____ _____
3. A community organization made up of small business owners and managers which assists small business owners .... _____ _____
4. A person who reviews leases and contracts .... _____ _____
5. A person who advises on means to protect assets in the event of accidents .... _____ _____

Activities

18-A. Choose a partner. Imagine that one of you is an SBDC advisor giving your client information about the following:
1. Writing a business plan
2. Types of assistance available through an SBDC (provide a brief description of each type of assistance)
3. Names of other sources of assistance (provide a brief summary of the function of each source)

In the space provided, make some brief notes about the types of SBDC assistance and the other sources of assistance you discussed with your partner.

Chapter 18   Name _____

18-B. Contact the nearest SBA office and your state's Department of Development and request a new business owner information package. Review the items you receive and determine which of them might be helpful to your hypothetical business. Make a list of these items and provide a brief description of how you might use them.

_____
_____
_____
_____
_____
_____
_____
_____
_____
_____
_____
_____

18-C. Ask an attorney and an accountant to review your business plan and give you a list of the legal/financial services that you might need. Using the lists they provide, fill in the information below.

Services needed now _____
_____
_____
_____

Services needed later _____
_____
_____
_____

Services not needed _____
_____
_____
_____

Chapter 18

18-D. Contact two or three insurance agents and obtain the following:
1. A complete list of the types of insurance coverage available to business owners and the estimated cost for each.
2. The agent's recommendations for the coverage you will need for your hypothetical business. (You will need to give the agent information about your business; have your business plan with you.)

Use the chart below to record information about the insurance you would need for your hypothetical business.

Coverage	Needed?	Cost
	Y / N	
	Y / N	
	Y / N	
	Y / N	
	Y / N	
	Y / N	
	Y / N	
	Y / N	
Total		

19 Special Regulations

Study Guide

Part A—*Directions:* In the answers column, write *T* if the statement is true or *F* if the statement is false.

1. Entrepreneurs enjoy a limited amount of freedom
2. The Federal Trade Commission advises businesses directly
3. Stores that seem to always be having a sale may attract the attention of the FTC
4. The FTC does NOT regulate consumer credit
5. Individuals cannot challenge the information in their credit reports
6. There are three types of warranties that are of concern to entrepreneurs
7. Sales talk can become an enforceable warranty
8. Warranties are sometimes important factors in buying decisions
9. It is a violation of federal law to offer a cash discount to customers who pay cash rather than using credit
10. Bills must be mailed at least 14 days in advance of their due date
11. The primary role of the Environmental Protection Agency is to prevent pollution
12. Retail businesses never have problems with the Environmental Protection Agency
13. Marital status, such as being divorced, is a legal reason to be denied credit
14. A warranty may be either written or verbal
15. Individuals have a right to have access to the information in their credit reports

Part B—*Directions:* In the blanks provided, write the word or phrase that best completes each sentence.

1. The federal administrative agency charged with responsibility for ensuring fair, free, and open business is called the _____.

2. Advertising containing information that would cause the average consumer to be misled about a particular product or service is called _____.

3. The practice of advertising a low-priced item as a means of luring customers into the store for the real purpose of selling them a higher priced item is _____.

4. The federal act that allows consumers access to their credit information is called the _____.

Chapter 19

5. Business owners offering credit must make credit available to all creditworthy customers regardless of race, national origin, marital status, religion, sex, age, or receipt of public assistance, according to the _____.

6. A clearly stated fact about the quality or performance of a product is a(n) _____.

7. Imposed by law, the _____ ensures that a product will perform whatever its function is under normal use and circumstances.

8. The act establishing standards for companies that choose to give written express warranties on consumer products is the _____.

9. The federal act that protects the public from dangerous products by providing evaluations of product safety hazards is called the _____.

10. The act stating that labels must warn consumers of the hazards of using products that may cause illness or death if improperly used is the _____.

Activities

19-A. Choose a well-known store in your community, or any store that you patronize regularly. Contact the local Better Business Bureau and ask whether there have been any consumer complaints about the business. Use the space below to make some notes about what you learn. Be prepared to discuss your findings in class.

Chapter 19　　　　　　　　　　　　　　　　　　　　　　　　　　Name _____

19-B. Look through your local newspaper. Cut out one or two advertisements that you think might be false or deceptive. In the space provided, explain why you think the advertisements may be misleading. Bring the advertisements to class for discussion.

_____
_____
_____
_____
_____
_____
_____
_____
_____
_____
_____

19-C. Find an example of a written product warranty. Does it meet the requirements of the Magnuson-Moss Warranty Act? Explain your answer in the space provided.

_____
_____
_____
_____
_____
_____
_____
_____
_____
_____
_____

Chapter 19

19-D. Go to a major retail chain store in your community. Ask for a credit application for a store credit card. Does it meet the requirements of the law? Look specifically for information that explains the complete costs of credit, including the annual percentage interest rate and finance charges. Explain your answers, and any concerns you may have, in the space provided. Be prepared to discuss the credit application in class.

20 Contracts and Agreements

Name _____

Study Guide

Part A—*Directions:* In the answers column, write *T* if the statement is true or *F* if the statement is false.

		Answers	For Scoring
1.	A contract is negotiated so that a promise or set of promises can be enforced by law	_____	_____
2.	A contract is usually negotiated between two or more persons	_____	_____
3.	A contractual offer must be intended to be legally binding	_____	_____
4.	Once communicated, an offer remains open until it is either accepted or rejected	_____	_____
5.	If the party receiving an offer makes a counteroffer, the original offer still stands	_____	_____
6.	An offer ends if either party is mentally incapacitated	_____	_____
7.	An acceptance may have special conditions attached	_____	_____
8.	Under certain circumstances, an acceptance is effective when it is mailed	_____	_____
9.	A contract may be legal even if completion of its terms is illegal	_____	_____
10.	One party to a contract must receive value	_____	_____
11.	Contract law does NOT require that consideration be equal	_____	_____
12.	Consideration may involve something that has already been done	_____	_____
13.	Consideration may be something that a person has a legal duty to do	_____	_____
14.	Past actions are not part of a legally enforceable contract	_____	_____
15.	There are no exceptions to the consideration requirement for a contract	_____	_____

Part B—*Directions:* In the blanks provided, write the word or phrase that best completes each sentence.

For Scoring

1. A legally enforceable agreement is a _____. _____

2. The communication of a proposal is called the _____. _____

3. When the receiving party agrees to an offer, it is called _____. _____

4. Value given and value received as a result of contractual agreement is _____. _____

5. The ability to fully understand and comprehend the requirements of a contract, as specified by law, is _____. _____

77

Chapter 20

6. A law that requires certain contracts to be written and signed is _____ _____.

7. Failure of a party to a contract to perform his or her obligation(s) as specified in the agreement is _____.

8. All parties are returned to their precontract condition and no damages are claimed in _____.

9. An injured party forces a breaching party to comply with the original terms of a contract in a _____.

10. The transfer of contractual rights to a party that was not part of the original agreement is called _____.

Activities

20-A. Bring at least one example of a contract to class. Identify the different elements of the contract. Make a few notes in the space provided about what you think the specific terms—and the contract as a whole—mean. Be prepared to discuss your ideas in class.

Chapter 20   **Name** _____

20-B. In your local newspaper, try to find at least one article that deals with some type of breach of contract. Make some notes in the space provided about the details of the case. Bring the article and your notes to class and be prepared to offer your opinion as to what the outcome will be.

Chapter 20

20-C. People are often in contractual situations even in their daily lives. Think back over the past week. List the situations you were in that would qualify as implied contracts. Bring the list to class and be prepared to discuss the various situations and their ramifications.

21 Buying and Selling

Study Guide

Part A—*Directions:* In the answers column, write *T* if the statement is true or *F* if the statement is false.

	Answers	For Scoring
1. The sale of land and services is covered under the regulations governing sales contracts	____	____
2. In general, when a contract is NOT for the sale of goods, common-law principles of contracts apply	____	____
3. General contract rules are applied in a more strict fashion for sales contracts	____	____
4. Sales contracts are not affected by types of sellers	____	____
5. The Uniform Commercial Code makes a distinction between the types of sellers	____	____
6. In a sales contract, a certain type of offer cannot be revoked	____	____
7. Consideration is NOT necessary to form a legally binding sales contract	____	____
8. Barter is a form of consideration	____	____
9. A firm offer of sale can be held open for six months without consideration	____	____
10. The exact amount of consideration must be included in a sales contract	____	____
11. The names of all of the people involved in the sales contract must be included on a written contract	____	____
12. In sales contracts, a reasonable price is determined by whatever price is customary in the industry	____	____
13. There is legal recourse for persons involved in illegal sales contracts	____	____
14. Sales contracts must be in writing	____	____
15. Sales contracts may be verbal	____	____
16. Risk of loss has no relationship to transfer of ownership	____	____
17. It is a good idea to address transfer of ownership specifically in sales contracts	____	____
18. If a sales contract allows a vendor to use third-party shipping, ownership transfers upon delivery of the merchandise to the shipper	____	____
19. When the purchaser picks up merchandise from the vendor, ownership remains with the vendor until the merchandise reaches the purchaser's place of business	____	____
20. In a cash and carry sale, ownership transfers once the merchandise reaches the customer's legal place of residence	____	____
21. In a C.O.D. sale, ownership transfers when the merchandise is given to the third-party deliverer	____	____
22. In a C.O.D. sale, the customer has no right of inspection prior to paying	____	____
23. In a sale on approval, ownership transfers when the merchandise arrives at the customer's legal place of residence	____	____
24. When vendors breach sales contracts, they lose all their rights	____	____
25. A purchaser may sue a vendor for specific performance in a breached contract situation	____	____

Chapter 21

Part B—*Directions:* In the blanks provided, write the word or phrase that best completes each sentence.

For Scoring

1. The immediate transfer of goods for a price is defined as a _____.

2. Items of tangible personal property other than money are called _____.

3. A group of uniform business rules adopted by most states is known as the _____.

4. In a sales transaction, the seller is known as the _____.

5. In a sales transaction, the buyer is known as the _____ or _____.

6. An individual who sells a particular good or goods on a regular basis and claims special knowledge is called a _____.

7. An individual who only sells occasionally and claims no special knowledge is called a _____.

8. A written, signed sales contract in which the merchant expresses the intention that it cannot be revoked is called a _____.

9. The amount of money, or consideration, agreed to by the parties to the sale is called the _____.

10. The term used when the sale involves only the exchange of goods is _____.

11. When one party to a sales contract has to bear the financial burden of damaged or destroyed goods or merchandise, that party bears the _____.

12. A sales transaction in which the buyer has the right to approve the merchandise prior to the transfer of ownership is called _____.

Part C—*Directions:* In the blanks provided, write the words or phrases that correctly complete each list.

For Scoring

1. List the three required terms of sales contracts.

   a. _____

   b. _____

   c. _____

Chapter 21 Name _____

2. List five terms that are permissible in sales contracts.

   a. _____ _____

   b. _____ _____

   c. _____ _____

   d. _____ _____

   e. _____ _____

Activities

21-A. In the newspaper, find and bring to class an example of a merchant's advertisement and an example of a casual seller's advertisement. Be prepared to discuss why you think the law views these types of sellers differently.

_____

_____

_____

_____

_____

_____

_____

_____

21-B. Find and bring to class an example of an offer for a sale on approval. What are the legal implications of the offer?

_____

_____

_____

_____

_____

_____

_____

_____

Chapter 21

21-C. Try to remember a sales transaction you have made during the last month that used barter as its form of consideration. Make some notes about the transaction in the space provided. Be prepared to discuss the specifics in class.

22
Real Property and Insurance

Study Guide

Part A—*Directions:* In the answers column, write *T* if the statement is true or *F* if the statement is false.

	Answers	For Scoring
1. An entrepreneur's ultimate goal is freedom	_____	_____
2. Property ownership is always the best choice for an entrepreneur	_____	_____
3. Buildings, as they relate to real property, are structures that are permanently attached to land	_____	_____
4. A movable shed would be considered a building	_____	_____
5. Once it is attached, a fixture becomes a part of real property	_____	_____
6. The purchase of real property requires a written contract	_____	_____
7. A bill of sale is a written document by which an individual conveys title and other rights of ownership of real property to another individual	_____	_____
8. Adverse possession is acquisition of another's land with permission	_____	_____
9. The required time of occupation for adverse possession is usually 5 to 20 years	_____	_____
10. Only a few states have community property laws	_____	_____
11. Easements are granted to keep someone from crossing the property of another	_____	_____
12. Assignment means to lease all or part of a leased property to a third party	_____	_____
13. Landlords may have the right to keep any fixtures that are added to a leased property	_____	_____
14. The concept of insurable interest was established to prevent profit from a situation in which there is no involvement	_____	_____
15. Any person may insure the life of another as long as the premium is paid	_____	_____

Part B—*Directions:* In the blanks provided, write the word or phrase that best completes each sentence.

For Scoring

1. Something that is owned or can be owned is _____. _____

2. Land, buildings, and fixtures are classified as _____. _____

3. "The solid portion of the earth's surface, a reasonable airspace above it, and anything that is located below it" is a definition of _____ in terms of real property. _____

4. A written document by which an individual conveys title and other rights of ownership of real property to another individual is a _____. _____

5. The kind of deed that transfers a seller's interest in real property with certain assurances is a _____. _____

Chapter 22

6. A deed that transfers whatever ownership interest the seller has to the buyer is a _____ _____.

7. Ownership by husband and wife, with rights of survivorship, is _____. _____

8. Property acquired during marriage is classified as _____. _____

9. A lease for a set period of time that will continue for similar periods of time until terminated is a _____. _____

10. A lease by which a tenant may remain in the facility after termination of the lease is a _____ _____. _____

Activities

22-A. Prepare a list of 20 items that you or your parents own. Indicate whether each item is real property or personal property. Be prepared to discuss your list in class.

_____
_____
_____
_____
_____
_____
_____
_____
_____
_____
_____
_____
_____
_____
_____
_____
_____
_____
_____
_____
_____
_____

Chapter 22 Name _____

22-B. Ask your parents or someone you know who owns property what form of ownership was chosen and why. Be prepared to discuss the information you obtain in class.

Chapter 22

22-C. Interview a business owner about the insurance coverage he or she carries for the business. For what reasons were the choices made? Be prepared to discuss the results of your interview in class.

23

Ethics and Social Responsibility in Entrepreneurship

Study Guide

Part A—*Directions:* In the answers column, write *T* if the statement is true or *F* if the statement is false.

	Answers	For Scoring
1. Ethics acceptable to management are rarely adhered to by employees	_____	_____
2. Even if all businesspeople maintained high ethical standards in the employment process, employment laws would still be necessary	_____	_____
3. Entrepreneurs should develop hiring policies based on ethics and the fair treatment of all applicants	_____	_____
4. Almost everyone has a set of moral standards..	_____	_____
5. Ethical treatment of competitors is not as important as ethical treatment of customers	_____	_____
6. Ethical treatment of consumers includes pricing, advertising, and warranties	_____	_____
7. The Federal Communication Commission has as its purpose the enforcement and monitoring of fair competition	_____	_____
8. An ethical entrepreneur will be forced by law to provide safe and comfortable working conditions for his or her employees	_____	_____
9. All entrepreneurs should try to minimize the negative impact of their business ventures on the environment	_____	_____
10. A code of ethics for today's entrepreneur should cover the treatment of consumers, the competition, and employees, as well as the use of computers	_____	_____
11. In relation to warranties, a good rule of thumb for the entrepreneur is to ask the question, "If I were the customer in this situation, would I think that I was treated fairly?"	_____	_____
12. Computer usage has a very clearly defined history of ethical values	_____	_____
13. Private enterprise can be effective without the guarantee of fair competition	_____	_____
14. Workplace ethics are often dictated by the work environment	_____	_____
15. Ethical advertising means not engaging in false advertising	_____	_____

Part B—*Directions:* List ten points contained within the Code of Ethics of the Association of Computing Machinery.

For Scoring

1. _____ _____

2. _____ _____

89

Chapter 23

3. _____ _____
4. _____ _____
5. _____ _____
6. _____ _____
7. _____ _____
8. _____ _____
9. _____ _____
10. _____ _____

Activities

23-A. Randomly pick ten individuals that you know. Ask them if they have ever used computer software illegally. Rephrase the question by asking if they have ever used or made copies of software programs. Report the results to your class.

_____
_____
_____
_____
_____
_____
_____
_____
_____
_____
_____
_____
_____
_____
_____
_____
_____

Chapter 23   Name _____

23-B. Contact a local retailer of computer software and interview a manager. Ask him or her to discuss the magnitude of illegal use of software and its impact on the company's profits.

_____
_____
_____
_____
_____
_____
_____
_____
_____
_____

23-C. Try to find a written warranty on a piece of retail merchandise. Examine the warranty and determine what it actually says, then decide what it actually means. Do you think there is a difference?

_____
_____
_____
_____
_____
_____
_____
_____
_____
_____

Chapter 23

23-D. Choose a small local company about which you have basic knowledge. Examine the demographics of its employees (race, age, sex, disabilities). Compare the company's demographics to those of your community in general. Is there a significant difference? If so, is there an explanation?

24
International Entrepreneurship

Study Guide

Part A—*Directions:* In the answers column, write *T* if the statement is true or *F* if the statement is false.

	Answers	For Scoring

1. Improvements in telecommunications and computer technology are responsible for small businesses being able to compete in today's international marketplace .... _____ _____
2. The United States currently has a trade deficit .... _____ _____
3. The International Trade Administration is a financial resource for international entrepreneurs. _____ _____
4. Businesses that market directly to overseas customers use foreign trading companies .... _____ _____
5. Licensing agreements allow a foreign business to use certain technological and intellectual properties of another business in exchange for a fee or royalty .... _____ _____
6. Eximbank's primary purpose is to provide overseas market information to exporters .... _____ _____
7. Receiving a letter of credit from a foreign buyer is considered a secure method of payment. _____ _____
8. NAFTA guarantees that only U.S.-made products will be sold in the U.S. .... _____ _____
9. Economic communities form when nations join together for mutual economic benefit .... _____ _____
10. Exports to former Soviet republics are expected to grow significantly in the future .... _____ _____
11. NAFTA is the largest trade agreement ever passed .... _____ _____

Part B—*Directions:* In the answers column, write the letter of the answer that best completes each statement.

	Answers	For Scoring

1. A country that imports more than it exports has a (a)trade surplus (b)trade deficit (c)favorable economic situation (d)growing employment base .... _____ _____
2. Opportunities for small businesses in international trade have improved as a result of (a)improved transportation facilities (b)lower long-term interest rates (c)improved telecommunication and computer technology (d)the efforts of the Small Business Administration .... _____ _____
3. Marketing directly to overseas markets (a)improves profit potential (b)is risky for small companies (c)gives the domestic business better control (d)all of the above .... _____ _____
4. Having a company that is already involved with a foreign market sell your product also is an example of (a)piggybacking (b)using an export management company (c)licensing (d)factoring. _____ _____
5. When a business has permission to use the technology of another business located outside its country, it is considered (a)a joint venture (b)a licensee (c)a franchise (d)a subsidiary .... _____ _____
6. An excellent government resource for financing export accounts receivable is (a)a commercial bank (b)a factoring house (c)Eximbank (d)the ITA .... _____ _____
7. A payment instrument that is guaranteed by the bank of the payee is a (a)letter of credit (b)bond (c)draft (d)voucher .... _____ _____
8. Fees imposed on imported goods are (a)sales taxes (b)drafts (c)commissions (d)tariffs .... _____ _____

93

Chapter 24

9. Factoring houses (a)are government sponsored (b)purchase accounts receivable below their actual value (c)are illegal (d)are used for start-up export companies .... _____ _____

10. The General Agreement on Trade and Tariffs (a)involved only the U.S., Canada, and Mexico (b)removed trade barriers between the U.S. and Canada (c)has existed since 1947 (d)regulates trade within the European community .... _____ _____

Part C—*Directions:* Match the following terms with their definitions. In the answers column, write the correct letter on the line next to each definition.

Terms

A. International Trade Administration
B. Eximbank
C. export management company
D. joint venture company
E. economic community

Definitions   Answers   For Scoring

1. A group of nations agree to cooperate in terms of tariffs, import quotas, and other trade concerns .... _____ _____
2. Assists in financing exporters' accounts receivable .... _____ _____
3. Acts as a partner in manufacturing goods overseas .... _____ _____
4. Provides important market information to exporters .... _____ _____
5. Assists in overseas marketing activities .... _____ _____

Activities

24-A. Learn about import/export opportunities either by reading articles in current periodicals or by interviewing someone knowledgeable about international trade. The person could be a government employee or a local businessperson currently engaged in international trade. Use the space provided either to take notes from your reading or to prepare your interview questions.

_____
_____
_____
_____
_____
_____
_____
_____
_____
_____

Chapter 24 Name _____

24-B. Survey the local market for imported products. Use the following list of countries and find at least one product imported from each.

Country **Product**

Mexico _____

Germany _____

Japan _____

England _____

Canada _____

Taiwan _____

China _____

Italy _____

France _____

Spain _____

Other _____ _____

24-C. Form a team of classmates with each member playing the role of a different member of an export chain. Designate (1) the manufacturer/exporter, (2) a representative from the ITA, (3) a commissioned agent or export management company representative, (4) an international banker, and (5) an importer. Create a hypothetical product and the activities necessary to sell the product overseas. In the space below, describe the role of each member in this process.

_____
_____
_____
_____
_____
_____
_____
_____
_____
_____
_____

Chapter 24

24-D. Visit a local manufacturing company that sells a product both domestically and internationally. Find out from the owner or manager whether there are any differences between how the company produces and markets the product for U.S. consumption and how it produces and markets the same product for overseas consumption. Write your findings in the space below.

25 Environmental Entrepreneurship

Study Guide

Part A—*Directions:* In the answers column, write *T* if the statement is true or *F* if the statement is false.

	Answers	For Scoring
1. There is general agreement about which environmental concern is the most threatening	_____	_____
2. Large businesses are leading the way in the recycling industry	_____	_____
3. In recent decades the public has become more aware of the environmental dangers that the world is facing	_____	_____
4. The general consensus is that we are currently doing enough to combat the environmental degradation of our planet	_____	_____
5. The quest for profits helped create our environmental crisis; entrepreneurs' quests for profits will encourage solutions to be found	_____	_____
6. A federal program, known as the Superfund, was established to finance the cleanup of our nation's most contaminated waste sites	_____	_____
7. The recycling rate for aluminum cans is more than 75 percent	_____	_____
8. The only limit to entrepreneurial opportunities relating to the environment is the imagination of individual entrepreneurs	_____	_____
9. A little over one-fourth of the motor oil used is actually recovered and recycled	_____	_____
10. Building materials recycling is an area that is saturated by creative and innovative approaches.	_____	_____
11. The business potential of plastics recycling is probably higher than any other area of recycling	_____	_____
12. Approximately 250 million tires are discarded every year in the U.S.	_____	_____
13. Approximately seven million cars are recycled every year in the United States	_____	_____
14. The current recycling rate for tires is around 40 percent	_____	_____
15. Air is the only channel for human exposure to hazardous waste	_____	_____

Part B—*Directions:* In the blanks provided, write the word or phrase that best completes each sentence.

For Scoring

1. Trash or garbage that cannot easily be recycled is _____.   _____

2. Air contaminated by combusting or burning fuels is _____.   _____

3. When chemicals or other hazardous substances invade water supplies or seep into underground water reserves, _____ occurs.   _____

4. Any waste product that poses a hazard to human health or the environment when it is improperly treated, stored, transported, disposed of, or otherwise managed is _____.   _____

97

Chapter 25

5. The process of transforming used and obsolete goods into useable and saleable goods is called _____.

6. The _____ of 1952 and the _____ of 1955 were the first two major statutes to regulate emissions of hazardous substances into the air and water.

7. The _____ of 1954 still regulates the handling and storage of radioactive wastes that are generated primarily at nuclear power reactors and federal nuclear weapons plants.

8. The _____ of 1974 was aimed at protecting the public from various contaminants in the drinking water supply.

9. The _____ of 1986 strengthened CERCLA and significantly increased its fund from $1.6 billion to $8.5 billion to clean up the nation's most contaminated hazardous waste sites.

10. The _____ of 1990 have increased the Environmental Protection Agency's power to impose much stricter control over a variety of air pollutants.

Activities

25-A. Read your local newspaper every day for a week. Each time you find an article about the environment, clip it out and bring it to class for discussion. Are there any differences between what you think are environmental issues and what your classmates consider environmental issues?

Chapter 25   Name _____

25-B. After reading the newspaper for a week, make a decision about what you think is the most critical environmental issue in your community. Be prepared to discuss and defend your choice in class.

_____
_____
_____
_____
_____
_____
_____
_____
_____
_____

25-C. Research three recycling businesses currently operating in your community. Be prepared to discuss the various types, their purpose, size, geographic territory, and any other information about them that you can determine.

_____
_____
_____
_____
_____
_____
_____
_____
_____
_____
_____
_____
_____
_____

25-D. Contact local government officials to determine the location and status of your local landfill. Status includes the expected number of years the landfill is to remain in use, restrictions on what can be put into it, the fees charged for its use, and any other pertinent information. If possible, visit the landfill site and report your observations to the class.